Reading takes practice and using materials like Unifix® Letter Cubes is a great way to have fun while learning. Use this bool Cubes along with Consonant-Vowel-Consonant Cubes.

Each activity presents a picture and word for the picture with the missing blend that is the activity's focus. Children see choices for the missing sound or blend and select the correct cube to build the word. They then put the word together and flip over the page to see the answer. Children should be encouraged to use cubes directly on the page but some prefer to look at the page and build words on the desk. Either way is fine. Other activities appear on the back, including additional words to build using the focus blend and some scrambled words. There may be more than one solution to the unscramble activities.

This book should be a good starting point for further activities on learning sounds and blends. The Unifix Letter and Blend cubes used with this book can be used in many ways in the home or classroom to stimulate reading skills. Just playing with the cubes helps children understand that letters and sounds are blended together to make words. Experimenting with changing the beginning and ending of words is another good way to learn about word families, sounds and phonics.

Ask your retailer or contact Didax for the following products to support this book:

DD2-810 Unifix Consonant-Vowel-Consonant Set, 90 Red and Blue Cubes; DD2-828 Unifix Blend Cubes, Set of 90

See back panel for all three books in this series. Didax, Inc. Rowley, Massachusetts 01969 USA Call 1-800-433-4329 for information or a dealer near you.

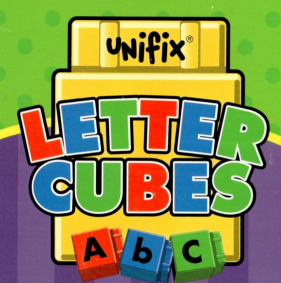

INITIAL BLENDS

AND DIGRAPHS

Didax
Educational Resources

UNIFIX®
LETTER CUBES
A b c

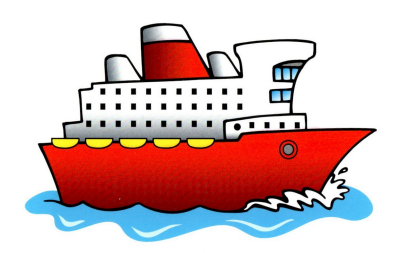

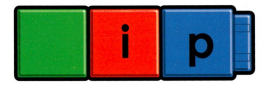

i p

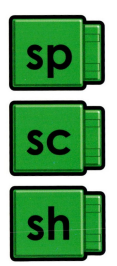

sp

sc

sh

1

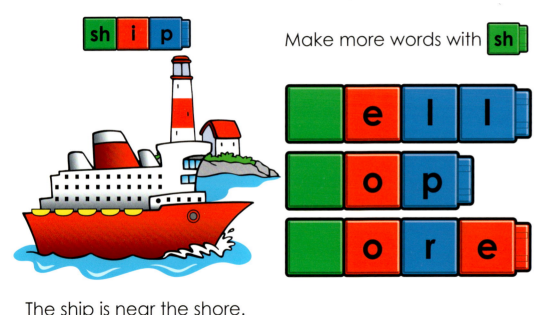

The ship is near the shore.

Make more words with **sh**

	e	l	l
	o	p	
	o	r	e

Can you find the words?

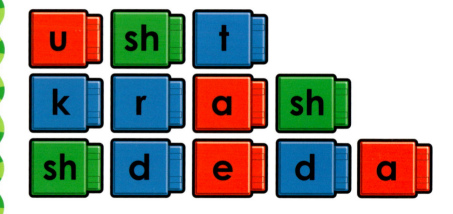

2

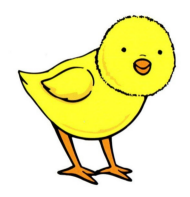

3

ch i c k

Make more words with ch

_ o p

_ i p

_ e s t

Can you find the words?

a t ch

ch r e e

i k c ch n e

A chick is a baby chicken.

4

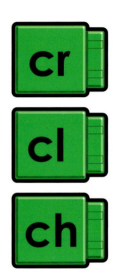

The clock in class says noon.

Make more words with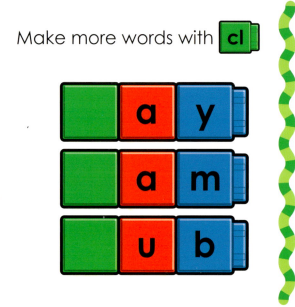

Can you find the words?

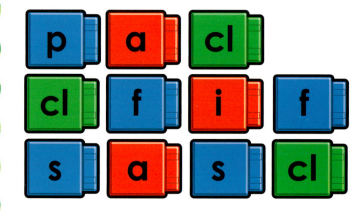

6

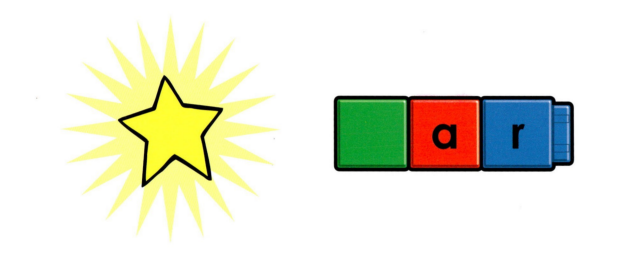

st **a** **r**

A star is on a stick.

Make more words with **st**

st **o** **p**

st **i** **c** **k**

st **a** **m** **p**

Can you find the words?

i	l	l	st
st	r	m	o
a	e	g	st

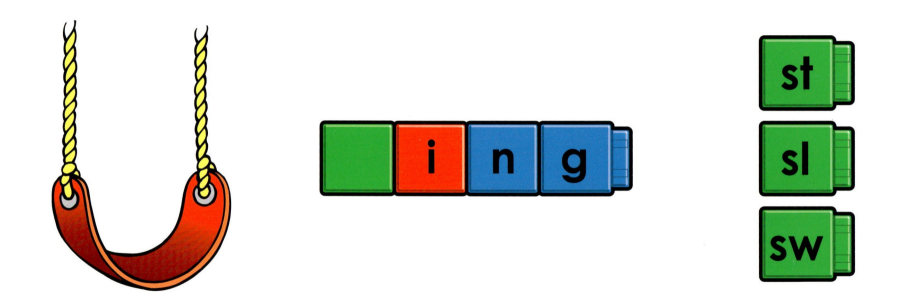

The swing is swell.

Make more words with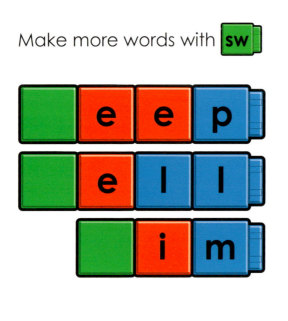

Can you find the words?

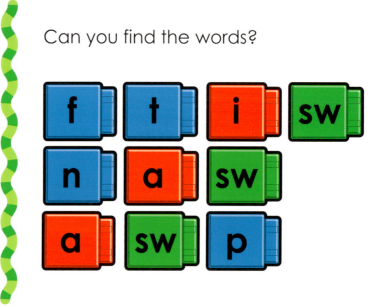

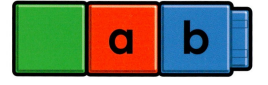

11

cr a b

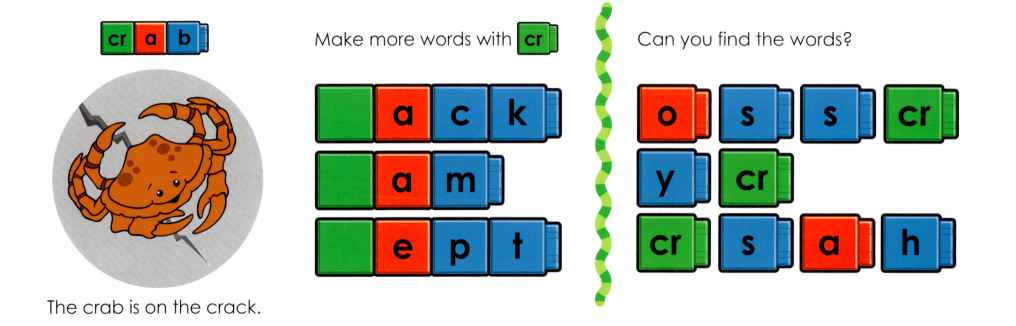

The crab is on the crack.

Make more words with cr

a c k

a m

e p t

Can you find the words?

o s s cr

y cr

cr s a h

12

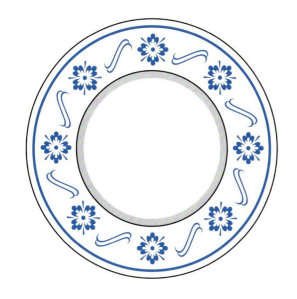

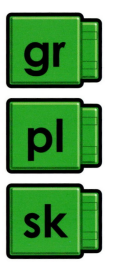

plate

The plant is on a plate.

Make more words with **pl**

	a	n
	u	m
	a	t	n

Can you find the words?

o pl p

y pl a

n e pl y t

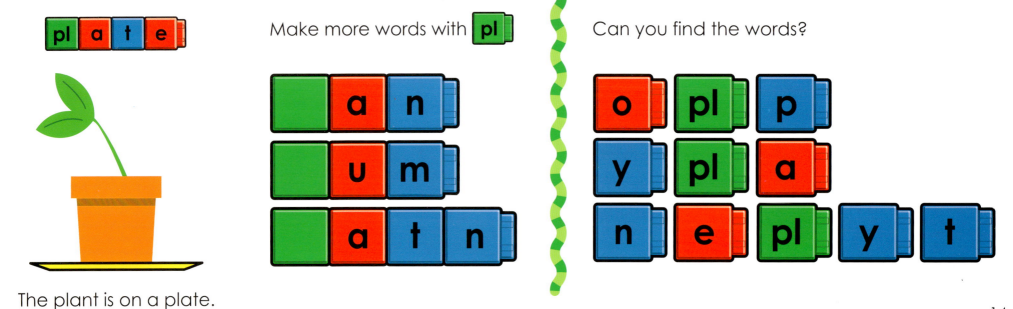

14

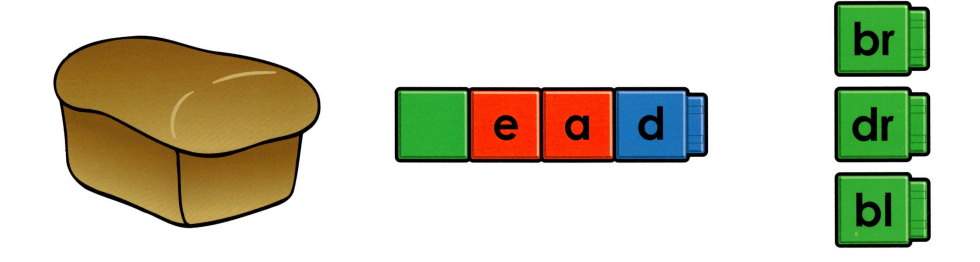

e a d

br

dr

bl

15

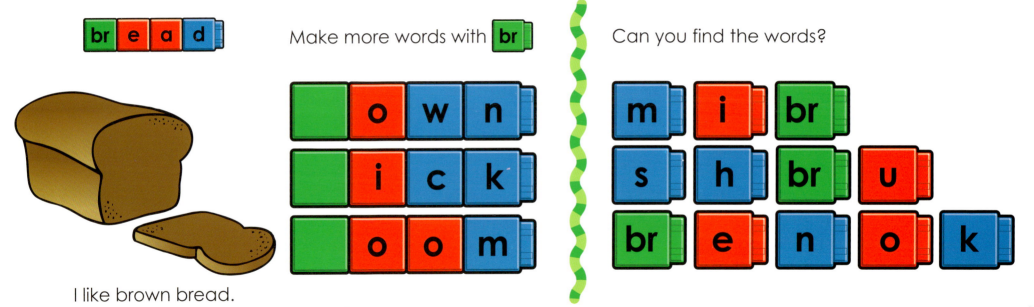

br **e** **a** **d**

I like brown bread.

Make more words with **br**

	o	w	n
	i	c	k
	o	o	m

Can you find the words?

m	i	br
s	h	br	u
br	e	n	o	k

16

sk a t e

Make more words with **sk**

Can you find the words?

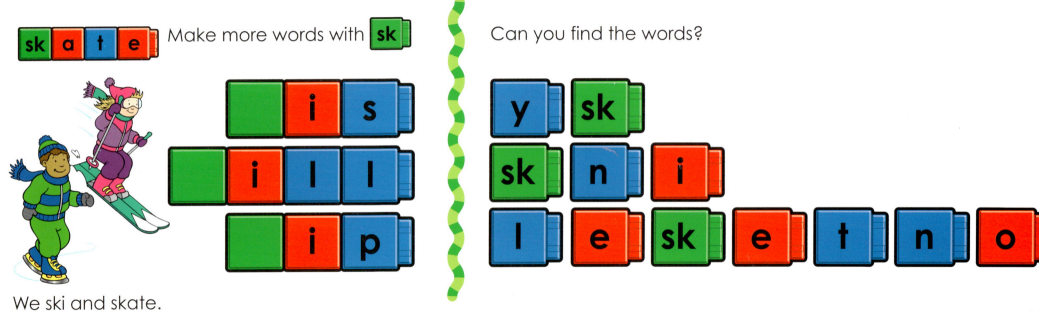

i s

i l l

i p

y sk

sk n i

l e sk e t n o

We ski and skate.

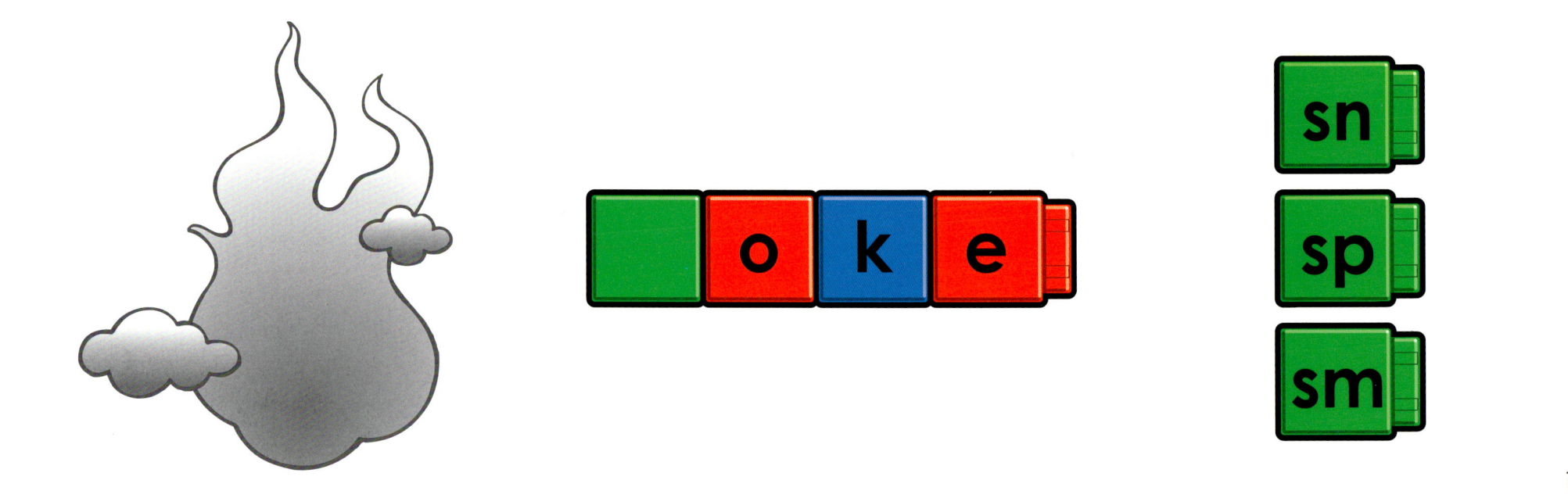

| o | k | e |

sn

sp

sm

smoke

Can you smell the smoke?

Make more words with **sm**

ell

ile

ock

Can you find the words?

g o sm
l a l sm
sm h a s

frog

The frog frowns.

Make more words with fr

y

o m

e e

Can you find the words?

t o n fr

fr t o s

w o fr n s

22

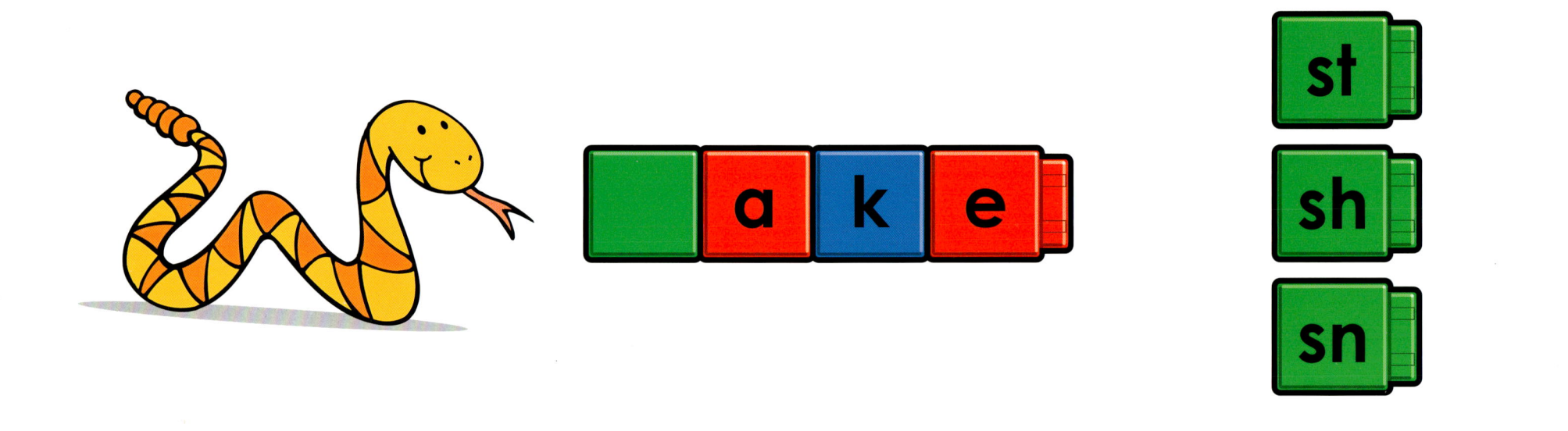

snake

This is a snug snake.

Make more words with sn

	u	g
	a	p
	o	w

Can you find the words?

f	i	f	sn
sn	o	p	o
z	o	o	sn	e

24

Look for the complete set of Unifix Letter Cubes Blend books

Donner

INITIAL BLENDS
AND DIGRAPHS
FLIP BOOK

Didax
Educational Resources

VOWEL SOUNDS
FLIP BOOK

Didax
Educational Resources

Didax

Educational Resources

Rowley, MA 01969
www.didaxinc.com

FINAL BLENDS
AND DIGRAPHS
FLIP BOOK

Didax
Educational Resources

ISBN 158324169-8

90000

9 781583 241691

2-830

Printed in USA.